Classic Motorcars
Coloring Book

by the Tre Tryckare Company

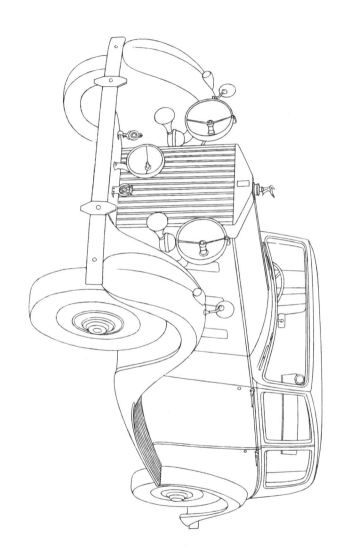

Dover Publications, Inc., New York

Publisher's Note

The era of the motorcar is generally considered to have begun in 1885, the year Gottlieb Daimler and Karl Benz independently of one another developed their first self-propelled vehicles. Since then car manufacturers worldwide have turned out thousands of makes of automobiles, most of which, in retrospect, were not particularly distinguishable from their contemporaries. Several makes, however, by virtue of the quality of their performance, the excellence and/or innovativeness of their design, or the significance of their historical impact, stood out from the rest. These are the cars we now know as classics. Regardless of their ages (the production lives of many classic motorcars ended long before many of us were born), their character, beauty and charm endure; existing specimens are still eagerly sought by collectors. These classic cars have the power to recall a time when driving was a pleasurable end in itself and not merely a means to an end, as it seems to be today.

This coloring book contains precise drawings of 46 classic European and American motorcars in chronological order, illustrating the technical and stylistic development of the automobile from around the turn of the century up to the early 1950s. Included are many of the automotive industry's best and most important cars: the luxurious Rolls-Royce Silver Ghost and Phantom III, Packard, Cadillac and Hispano-Suiza; the best-selling Austin 7, Morris Oxford, Ford Model T and Model A, Citroën and Volkswagen; the fast and sporty Sunbeam, Talbot-Lago, M.G. Midget, Alfa-Romeo and XK 120 Jaguar; the innovative Lanchester, Essex Coach, Lancia Lambda and Pierce-Arrow Silver Arrow; and many more.

All the illustrations are eminently suitable for coloring. If you want to retain all the printed lines, it is best to use transparent washes, felt-tip pens or colored pencils. Though the drawings abound in interesting details, it is not necessary to color each small area separately. Large sections of these cars were uniform in color. The examples on the covers, rendered in authentic period coloring, are an excellent guide to the distribution of tones and values.

Published in Canada by General Publishing Company, Ltd., 30 Lesmill Road, Don Mills, Toronto, Ontario.

Classic Motorcars Coloring Book, first published by Dover Publications, Inc., in 1986, is a new selection of 46 illustrations (all previously published elsewhere) by the firm Tre Tryckare AB. The text was prepared specially for the present edition, which is published by special arrangement with AB Nordbok, Göteborg (Gothenburg), Sweden.

International Standard Book Number: 0-486-25138-1

Manufactured in the United States of America
Dover Publications, Inc., 31 East 2nd Street, Mineola, N.Y. 11501

1. "Seventy Panhard," 1902. The French Panhards were among the most successful racing cars in the world after the turn of the century. This 1902 model, however, was more famous for its huge 4-cylinder, 70-hp, 13.5-liter engine than for its racing exploits. Faster than its smaller competitors on straight roads, the "Seventy" was ill equipped to handle the winding roads over which most races were run.

2. Lanchester, 1904. The English twin-cylinder Lanchester, first produced in 1901, was truly an original and influential car. It was the first automobile in production that was designed as a unit and not as an assemblage of distinct components. The streamlined appearance of the open-tonneau body on this 1904 model was in direct contrast to the stumpy, boxy look prevalent at the time. Other design innovations, including its rigid chassis with soft-spring suspension and its vibrationless 12-hp engine, gave the Lanchester a ride that was unequaled for many years.

3. F.N., 1910. Around the turn of the century, many firms in engineering-related fields branched out into the burgeoning automotive industry. This finely crafted 12-hp automobile was a product of the Fabrique Nationale d'Armes de Guerre, a Belgian armaments firm. The car's body resembles those used on racing cars of that period, but this little runabout's top speed was only 50 mph.

4. 40/50 Silver Ghost Rolls-Royce, 1910. Considered by many to be the best car ever built, the 40/50 was easily the most famous of all the early luxury automobiles. Its finest feature was its silent ride—it was "quiet as a ghost." Designed in 1906, this model remained in continuous production with only minor variations until 1924. Employing a virtually noiseless and vibrationless 7.5-liter, 6-cylinder, 48-hp engine, the 1910 model of this English classic could exceed 65 mph in top gear.

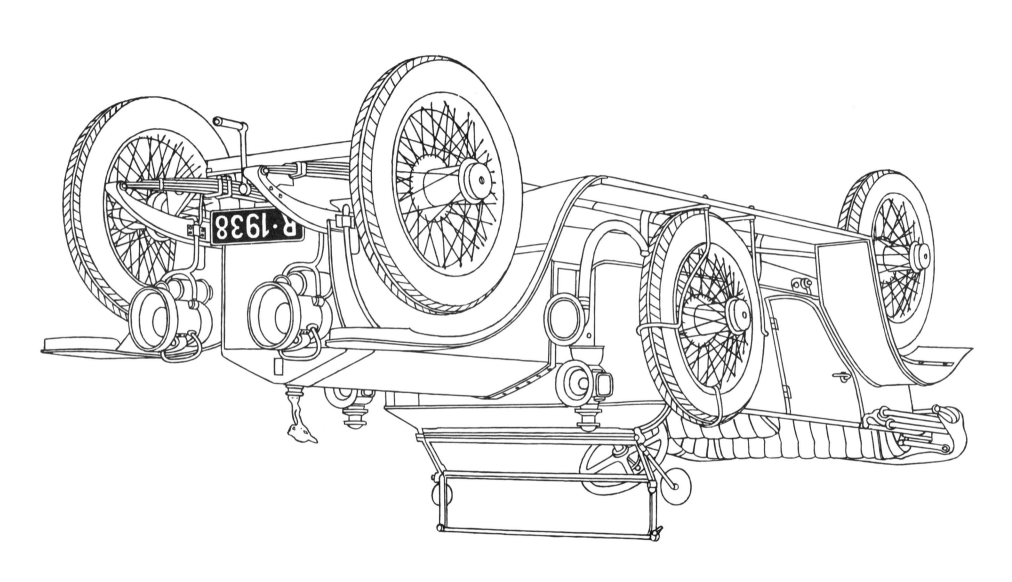

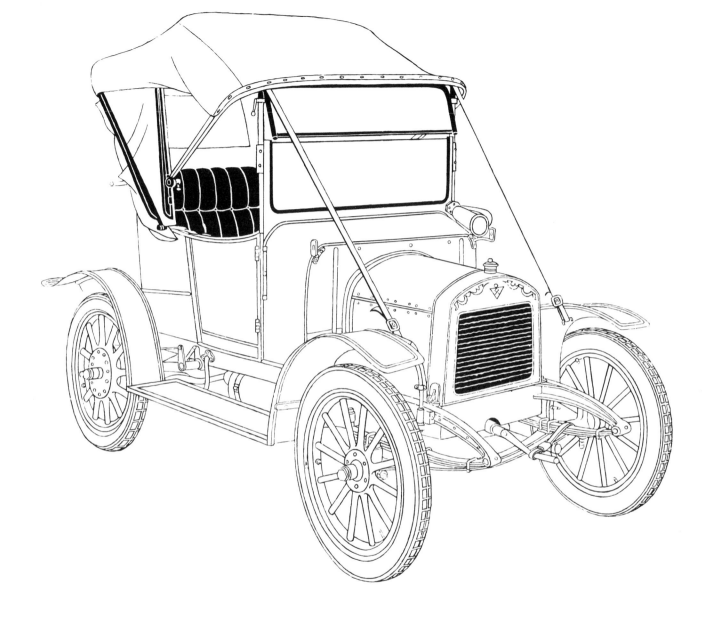

5. Austin 7, 1911. Forerunner of the famous Austin cars of the 1920s and 30s, this 1-cylinder, 3-speed, 7-hp motorcar, along with similar small, low-powered, relatively inexpensive automobiles, brought motoring to the middle class. It also typified the somewhat piecemeal way that most early motorcars were constructed and bought. The manufacturer offered a chassis at a set price; the buyer then had to select and pay extra for the body of his choice. The body might have been made by the car builder or by an outside coach-building firm. To the body then would be attached the hood, tires, windshield, doors and other essentials, each paid for separately. The body shown here was but one of many built by Austin to fit this chassis.

6. Napier, 1912. Although the British Napier was best known in its 6-cylinder form, the smaller 4-cylinder, 12-hp version, like the touring model shown here, was very popular among motorists who wanted a smooth, quiet ride, precise controls and the benefits of expert construction without the high price of the larger engine. The Napier was one of the first cars to feature an engine and gearbox that were constructed as a unit, making it nearly impossible for them to get out of alignment.

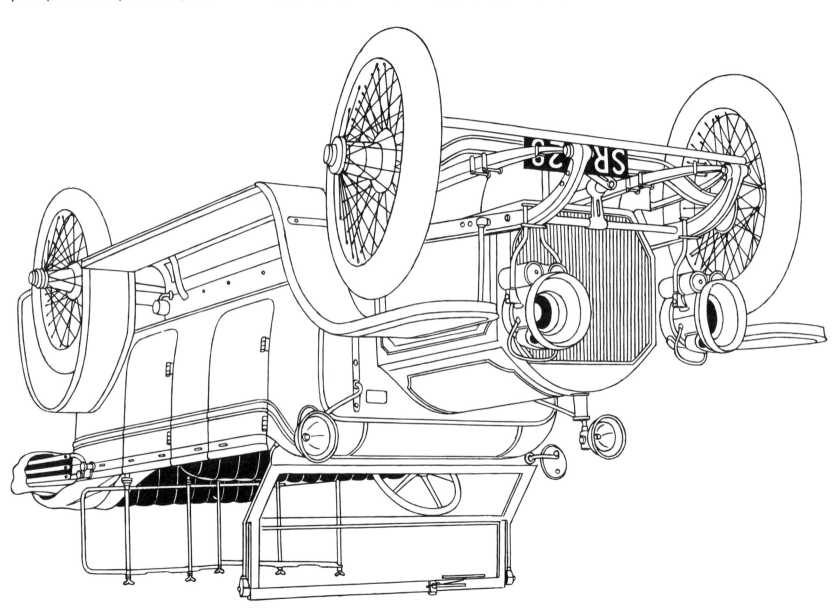

7. Morris Oxford, 1913. The foremost light car of its day, the "Bullnose Morris" combined quality and ease of driving with reasonable cost. First produced in 1913, this British motorcar remained in production for fourteen years. Unlike other cars of the period, the standard 8.9-hp Morris came from the manufacturer fully equipped; therefore, the prospective buyer did not have to calculate the cost of each accessory to determine the total price of the automobile.

8. Rolls-Royce Continental, 1914. Although this slightly modified version of the standard 40/50 Silver Ghost was officially called the Continental by the company, it was better known to most as the "Alpine Eagle." In 1913 a car of this type won the famous Austrian Alpine Trial, an arduous race of over 1,650 miles through the Austrian Alps. The Continental differed from earlier models in that its power output had been increased. The 1914 model was capable of 80 mph, and its ride was as smooth and quiet as ever.

9. Sunbeam, 1914. Throughout automotive history, many of the most significant advances in engine efficiency were designers' responses to demands by racers for more power from smaller, lighter engines. The Sunbeam Company's renowned torpedo-shaped Grand Prix racing car incorporated many of the latest design innovations of its day. Its British-built engine was able to develop over 30 bhp per liter, five times the power output of the best engines only fourteen years earlier.

10. Arrol-Johnston, 1917. When World War I began in 1914, the building of private automobiles in Europe virtually stopped, as car manufacturers turned their attention to the making of munitions. The few companies that continued to produce nonmilitary motorcars did so for the most part without drastically altering existing prewar designs. Modifications that were instituted during the war years were primarily cosmetic. Produced in 1917, this Scottish-made Arrol-Johnston was identical to prewar models except that its hood had been redesigned to accommodate the fitting of the radiator in front of the engine rather than behind it. Its production life was brief, though, technically advanced designs replacing it when full-scale production recommenced after the war.

11. Citroën Type A, 1919. As soon as the First World War was over, demand for inexpensive, reliable cars increased rapidly. In France André Citroën, previously a gear manufacturer, entered the automotive industry in 1919 with the Type A, the first of a long line of sturdy and reliable models Citroën was to produce. Electric lighting and pressed-steel wheels were features of this straightforward touring car.

12. Essex Coach, 1922. In the United States, car production continued virtually without interference during the years of the First World War, and during that time considerable advances were made in the perfection of the all-steel car body. By 1916 an open touring body made entirely of pressed steel was being turned out in great quantity in America. The 1922 Essex Coach made history as one of the first low-cost all-steel-body cars with a solid roof offered in the States.

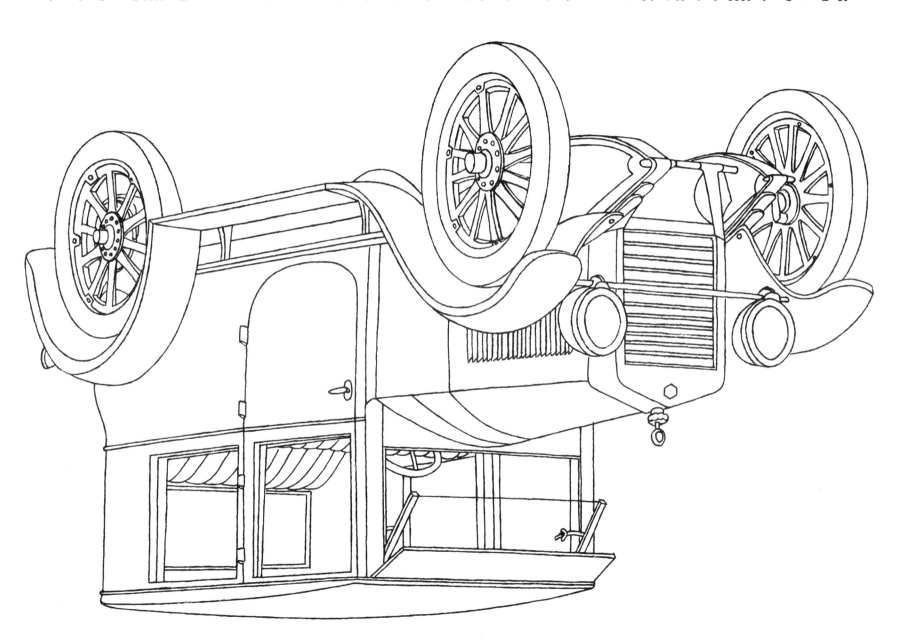

13. Model T Ford, 1924. Henry Ford was a pioneer of mass-production in the automotive industry, and, more than any other individual, was responsible for popularizing the motorcar. At a time when other car manufacturers were producing several cars a week, the Ford Motor Company was using a moving-line type of assembly to turn out as many as a thousand Model T bodies a day. First introduced in 1908, the Model T remained in production basically unchanged for over nineteen years. By 1927 more than fifteen million had been built, and its place in automobile history had been firmly established. Its low purchase price, its ability to go seemingly anywhere and its ease of driving, maintenance and repair made motoring possible for almost everyone in America and worldwide. The 1924 model, pictured here, offered no suggestion of the luxury found in many other cars of that period, but, like every other version of the "Tin Lizzie," it provided maximum reliability at minimum cost.

14. Lancia Lambda, 1925. The design of the Italian Lancia Lambda was years ahead of its time. Introduced in 1922, the Lambda was one of the first automobiles to feature unitary construction of its chassis and body. To this one-piece frame only the doors, hood, fenders and some paneling had to be added. Unitary construction, despite its overwhelming advantages, was not put into practice by most European manufacturers until the mid-1930s. Other significant mechanical breakthroughs introduced by the Lambda included independent front-wheel suspension and front-wheel brakes. The Lambda's compact, narrow-V-formation, 4-cylinder engine produced 50 hp and propelled the car at speeds of over 70 mph.

15. Renault, 1926. Despite the increased demand following World War I for smaller, cheaper cars, large, beautifully finished, expensive automobiles were still popular. Those who could afford to continued to demand cars of the highest quality; thus, the tradition of large, hand-built motorcars with individually fitted components persisted. One of the most impressive cars of the 1920s was the large-engined, 140-hp Renault. This French-built automobile had a 9.1-liter engine mounted in front of the radiator, could exceed 80 mph and was big enough to carry the most luxurious body types. Here it is shown with an open torpedo body, one of the most attractive styles made by the coach-building firm Billancourt.

16. Alvis 12/50, 1926. The vintage years from 1919 to 1930 saw the always popular sports car reach its height in development. One of the best and most famous sports tourers of this period was the British Alvis 12/50. It was highly reliable and economical, and offered the dash and performance of a racing car combined with the comfort and grace of a standard touring car. Capable of traversing difficult routes at high speeds, the well-handling 12/50, unlike many cars, was fun to drive.

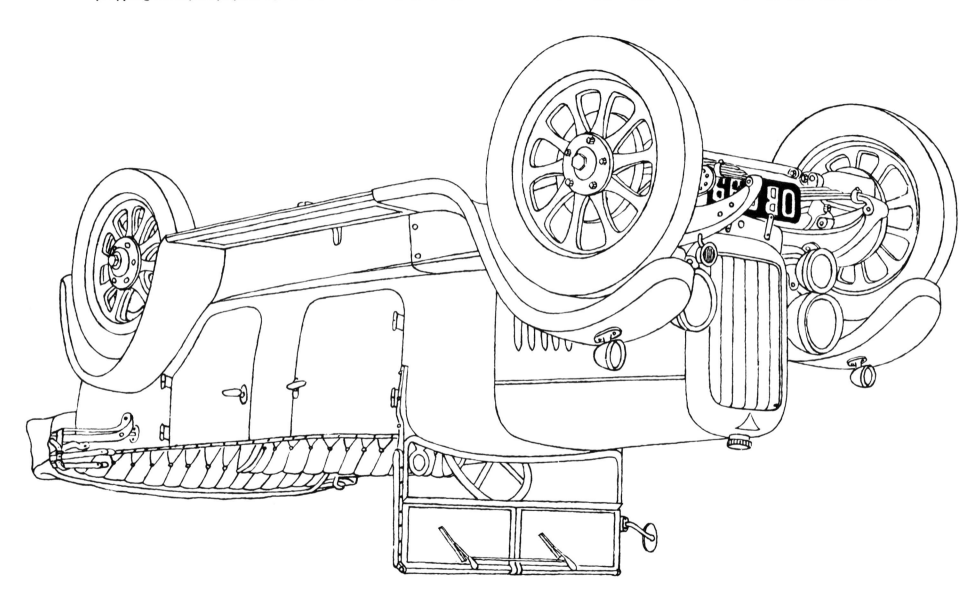

17. Model A Ford, 1928. By 1927 the Model T Ford had become antiquated. Rather than update the Model T design, Henry Ford decided to replace it with the completely new Model A. Shown here in its original 1928 roadster form, the Model A, like the Model T, was a universal car; over five million were built throughout the world. Its 3.3-liter, 4-cylinder engine produced 40 hp and provided speeds up to 65 mph.

18. 37.2 Hispano-Suiza, 1928. Founded around the turn of the century in Barcelona by a Swiss engineer, the firm of Hispano-Suiza has produced some of the world's greatest cars, many of which have even challenged the Rolls-Royce for world supremacy. The famous 37.2-hp, 6.5-liter Hispano-Suiza was constructed at the Hispano works in France. It was a splendid, expensive motorcar bought by royalty and the most particular connoisseurs. Its elegance, comfort, road-handling qualities and performance were unmatched in its day, except perhaps by the Rolls-Royce Phantom I.

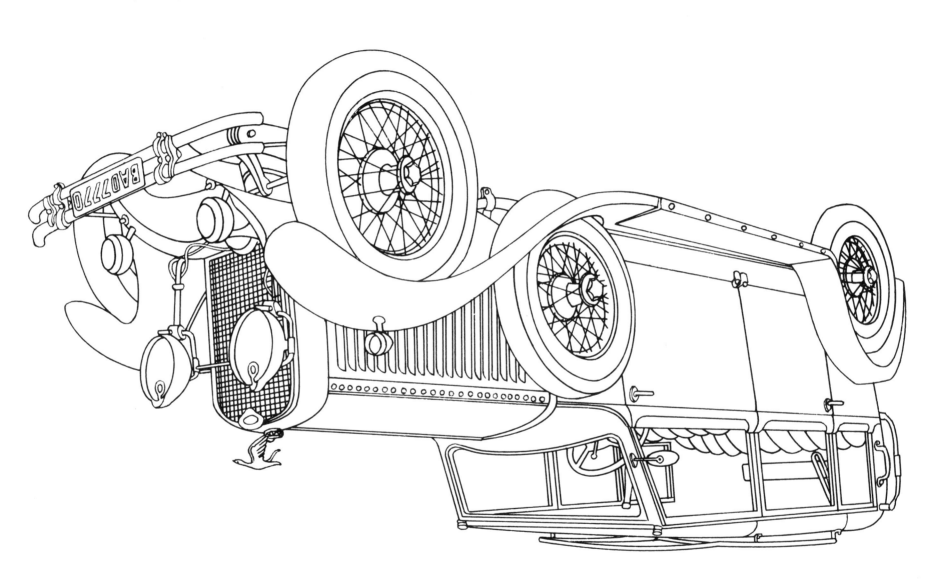

19. Daimler 12/70, 1928. Many of the most luxurious and best-looking coachbuilt bodies ever crafted were products of designers from the late 1920s and early 30s. In order to handle these grand bodies, the chassis to which they were fitted had to be amply large and powerful. The many models of chassis and engines produced by the British firm Daimler were particularly well suited, both physically and aesthetically, for even the most impressive types of body that might be fitted. Daimler chassis were powered by a quiet and sturdy Knight sleeve-valve type of engine, and their tall radiators and long, high hoods gave them an attractive up-to-date look. Here the 12/70 model has been fitted with an open sporting body by Hooper & Company.

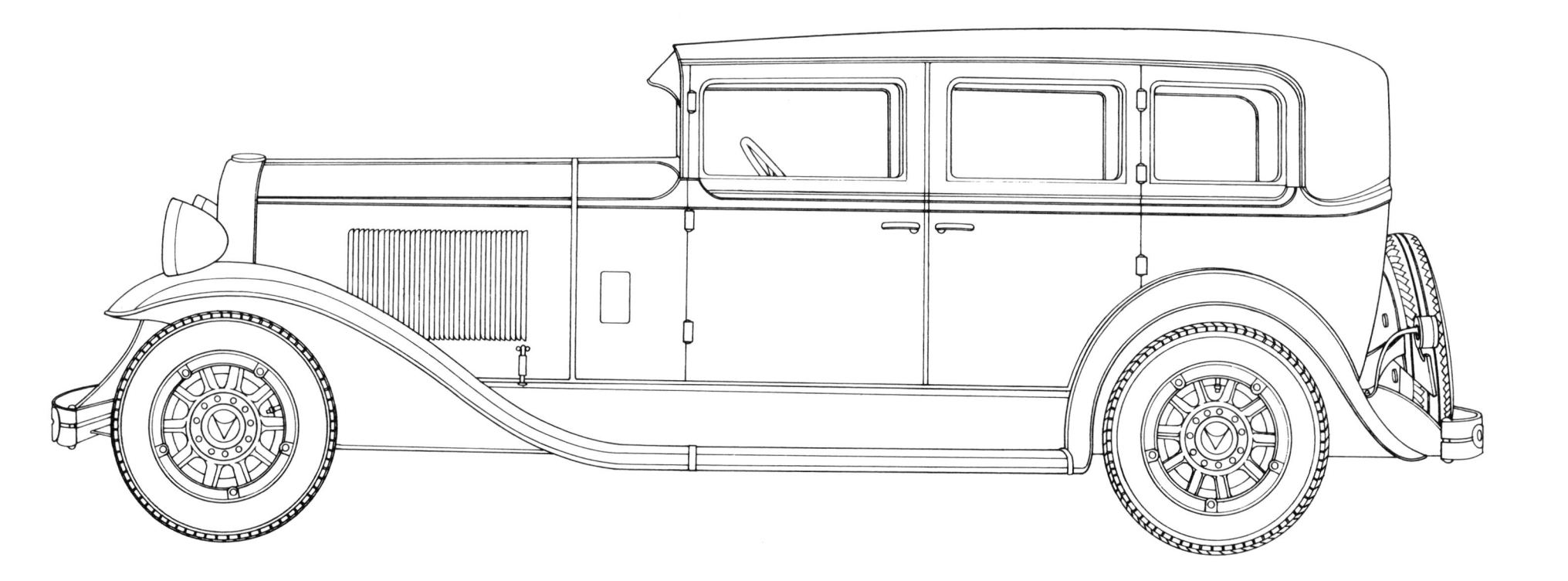

20. Oldsmobile Viking, 1929/30. The Viking was an ingenious, innovative automobile that had an advanced, top-of-the-line, V-8, 4.2-liter, 81-hp engine capable of outperforming similarly priced competitors. Introduced in April 1929, the Viking was intended to boost Oldsmobile's already impressive sales; instead it was a flop. Because of the Depression, the Viking never got off the ground, lasting only until the autumn of 1930 and selling only 8,000 units.

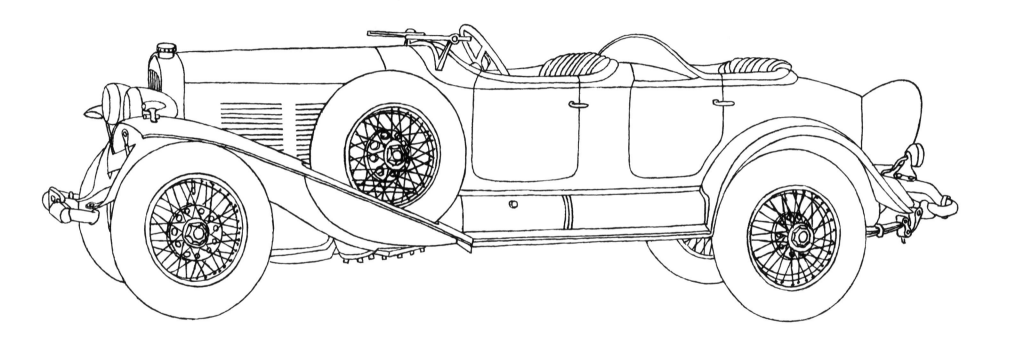

21. Lincoln Phaeton, 1929. The V-8 engine of the Lincoln was in continuous production from 1920 until 1931. In its 1929 form it developed 90 hp and was exceptionally refined in operation. Considering Henry Ford's succcess with the Model T and Model A, it is not surprising that Ford-owned companies, like Lincoln, were reluctant to alter effective existing designs significantly. Lincoln's continued financial success testified to the soundness of its conservative policy. The sporty polished-aluminum body of this Phaeton was made by Le Baron.

22. Crossley 15.7, 1929. A body type that enjoyed immense popularity from the late 1920s onward was the sportsman's coupé sedan. It was shorter and somewhat less spacious than the standard sedan but had a more pleasing and dignified appearance. The body on this British-built, 6-cylinder, 15.7-hp Crossley, with its tall radiator and removable roof, was typical of the style.

23. Fiat 9, 1930. During the late 1920s and early 30s, most low-priced motorcars were similar in that they were enclosed, mass-produced and made of pressed steel. This 1930 Fiat 9 was typical. Its boxy shape, dictated in part by the limitations of the as yet largely unrefined manufacturing process, exemplified the shape of inexpensive cars of all makes throughout Europe. At 22 hp, the two-door sedan was the smallest model offered at the time by Fiat, Italy's premier car manufacturer.

24. M.G. Type M, 1930. Though somewhat diminished, demand for the open touring type of bodywork still persisted in the 1930s, mostly in the sports-car field. This M-type M.G., the company's first Midget, was a successful sports car, offering surprising power at a very reasonable price. Its 4-cylinder engine produced a mere 20 hp, but remarkably could propel the car at speeds of over 60 mph. Though lacking luxuries found on many larger British sports cars, the Type M, like M.G.'s entire Midget line, was extremely popular with sporting enthusiasts for its performance, handling and unique character.

25. Pierce-Arrow Silver Arrow, 1933. The Silver Arrow was years ahead of its time, especially in its outward appearance. With its streamlined fenders, rounded roof line and contained headlamps, it anticipated styling fashions that would be popular fifteen years later. First introduced by the small American firm Pierce-Arrow in 1933, the very expensive Silver Arrow had a large V-12 engine that produced 175 bhp. Despite its advanced design and superb performance and handling, its production life was extremely short because of the financial difficulties of its makers.

26. Frazer Nash Le Mans Replica, 1934. Few sports cars ever *looked* as fast as the Frazer Nash. Unlike many sporting cars, it was not simply a modified version of a standard touring model; it was built by the small British firm Frazer Nash specifically for sports driving. It carried no extra luxuries; every compo- nent was designed for speed and performance. As a result, the Nash was a small, fast, highly responsive machine that was enormously satisfying to drive. This model had a 4-cylinder Meadows engine, and its final drive to the rear wheels was by chains.

27. Renault with Fernandez *Coupé-Chauffeur* Sedanca Coachwork, 1934. Owing in large part to the Depression, the 1930s saw a sharp decline in the number of specialist coachbuilders. Factory-built or factory-commissioned bodies offered more than adequate luxury for most car buyers and cost less than custom-built coaches. However, a small demand for elegant custom coachwork still persisted. Pictured here is an extravagant 1934 *coupé-chauffeur* sedanca built by Fernandez of France and fitted on Renault's straight-eight chassis. The sedanca type of body reached its zenith in the 1930s but declined thereafter. Strictly chauffeur-driven, it was permanently closed over the rear seats and had a cover over the front seats that could be removed.

28. Standard 10/12, ca. 1935. The British firm Standard-Triumph, one of the few manufacturers of large nonluxury cars to survive the economic problems of the late 1920s and early 30s, firmly established itself in the public's favor with reliable models such as this midsize sedan, the 10/12. Mass-produced, rela-tively inexpensive and with low fuel consumption, this 4-door Standard sold well even during the Depression years. Though lacking most luxuries, the 10/12 did feature as standard equipment windshield wipers and a trunk for the spare tire, both fairly recent innovations.

29. Buick Special, 1936. By the mid-1930s, the automotive industry had become a very specialized field of business. Companies, for the most part, exclusively built one, possibly two types of automobiles. The big volume producers made small, inexpensive vehicles that appealed to the masses; other manufacturers built midsize cars for the family-oriented middle class; and makers of luxury cars and specialist automobiles, such as sports cars and limousines, catered to the demands of the wealthy. Large mass-production-based combines made up of several specialized branches needed to produce motorcars that appealed to most segments of the market in order to be successful. The largest of these combines in the United States was, and still is, General Motors, which saturated the market with everything from the low-priced Chevrolet up to the Cadillac. Oldsmobile, Pontiac and Buick were divisions of GM that produced midsize automobiles. This roomy Buick Special, "the Doctor's Friend," so called because the car's reliability and elegant—but not ostentatious—appearance made it a popular choice among doctors and other professionals, demonstrates the style of body that dominated the midsize and luxury lines of motorcars in the 1930s. Designers eliminated all visible sharp angles to achieve this streamlined compound-curve style.

30. 4-Liter Talbot-Lago, 1937. It was not unusual for automotive firms that specialized in manufacturing racing cars to turn out conventional road cars as well. The Anglo-French firm of Talbot produced several racing cars that dominated their classes, but was probably better known for its successful line of semi-luxury fast tourers in the late 1930s. The race-bred 4-liter Talbot-Lago pictured here combined elegant coachwork with a light, compact frame and a twin-carburetor, 6-cylinder engine that produced 140 bhp at 4,000 rpm, making it one of the sharpest-looking motorcars on the road, capable of cruising at speeds approaching 100 mph.

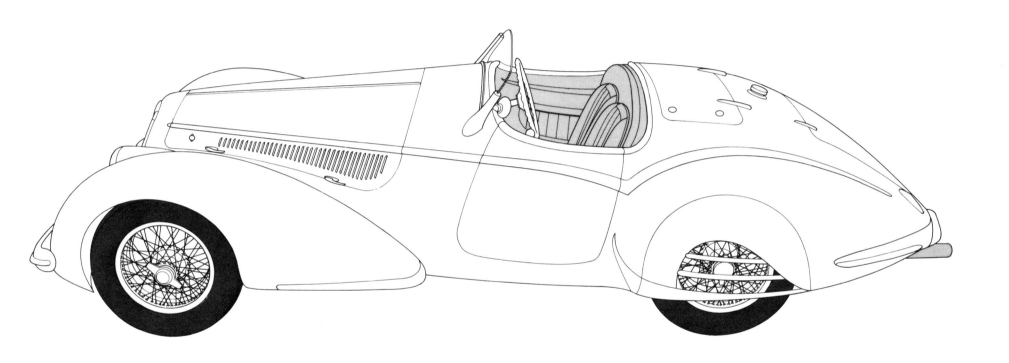

31. Alfa-Romeo 8C 2900B, 1938. Probably the fastest sports car one could buy between the years 1937 and 1940, the Alfa-Romeo 8C 2900B was also one of the rarest. Its genesis was unique: In 1938 Alfa-Romeo, an Italian firm, had on hand thirty-five surplus 8-cylinder engines originally built for its by-then-defunct 1935 Grand Prix racing car. After being detuned, these engines were placed into independently sprung chassis and enclosed by smooth, sleek bodies. The result was a limited number of top-of-the-line, very expensive, very responsive sports cars with a top speed of 130 mph.

32. DKW, 1938. A product of the great German Auto Union Company, this front-wheel-drive motorcar was noticeably spacious for a car of just over 20 hp. It was powered by a twin-cylinder, 2-stroke engine that had only five moving parts and was so flexible it could go from 6 to 60 mph in top gear. With a fuel consumption of 55 mpg, the 1938-model DKW was extremely economical to operate.

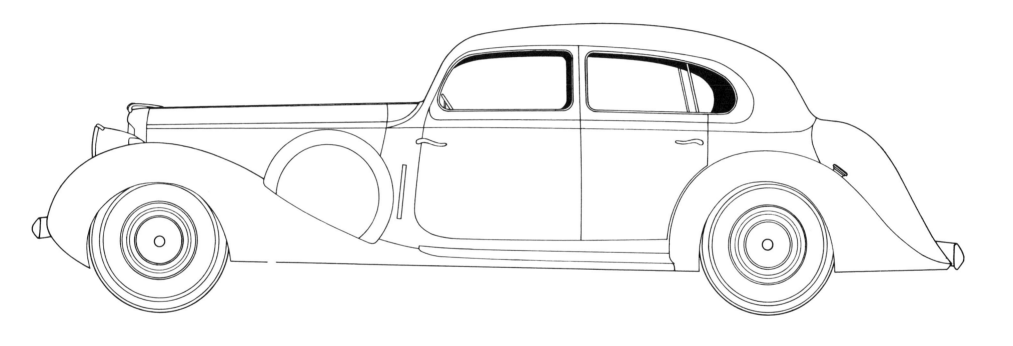

33. Lagonda De Ville, 1938/39. Although its brief prewar run allowed little time for refinement, this British V-12 Lagonda was one of the finest large motorcars of any period. Its 4.5-liter, 180-bhp engine could propel the two-ton car at speeds approaching 100 mph. Though the elegant De Ville featured limousine bodywork, its superb road-handling ability and sporty looks often lured its owners to take the wheel themselves rather than be driven in it.

34. 3.5-Liter S.S. Jaguar, 1939. When the British producers of S.S. cars introduced their first Jaguar model in 1935, they gained a well-deserved reputation for offering one of the best values ever seen in the automotive industry. The Jaguar was an exceptional high-performance vehicle offered at a relatively low price. Succeeding models only strengthened that reputation. For the 1939 season, their largest model, shown here, had a 3.5-liter, 25-hp engine that provided ample power to handle its spacious and fully equipped sedan body. This model was capable of traveling at 90 mph with reasonable economy.

35. Rolls-Royce Phantom III, 1939. Design work on the Phantom III, the last of the line of 40/50 Rolls-Royces that began in 1906 with the Silver Ghost, started in 1932 and was completed in 1936, the year the car was first introduced. Between then and the outbreak of the Second World War, only 710 units were made. It was one of the most expensive motorcars in the world and, like its predecessors, offered a smooth, quiet ride and a performance that was unrivaled. It employed a V-12 engine and had a top speed of over 100 mph. The Phantom III, as has every succeeding Rolls-Royce model, set the standard by which all other luxury automobiles are judged.

36. Allard Special V-12, 1939. The high prices of the grand European luxury cars prohibited all but the very rich from owning them. However, the decade prior to the Second World War saw several attempts to achieve motorcars of comparably high quality at lower cost. The most successful of these were the sporting Anglo-Americans, fast cars that combined British chassis and styling with large, relatively inexpensive American engines. The British-built Allard Special was fitted with several American components, including, in this case, a V-12 Lincoln-Zephyr engine. A Ford engine could also be ordered if desired. This large, powerful, custom-built open sports car was ideally suited for the sport of rallying, for which this particular model was commissioned.

37. Volkswagen KdF-Wagen, 1939. This 1939 KdF-Wagen was the forerunner of the Volkswagen Beetle, one of the most popular and best-selling automobiles of all time. First produced in 1939, the KdF had a very short run; only 210 were completed before Volkswagen's factory was changed over to war production. Like its famous successor, it was small, inexpensive, sturdy, reliable and easy to maintain and service. Its 985-cc engine was located in the car's rear and could propel the car over 60 mph. The "bug"-shaped body on the KdF, first designed by Dr. Ferdinand Porsche in 1932, changed very little throughout the long production life of the Beetle series, a life that saw over eighteen million of these endearing cars built.

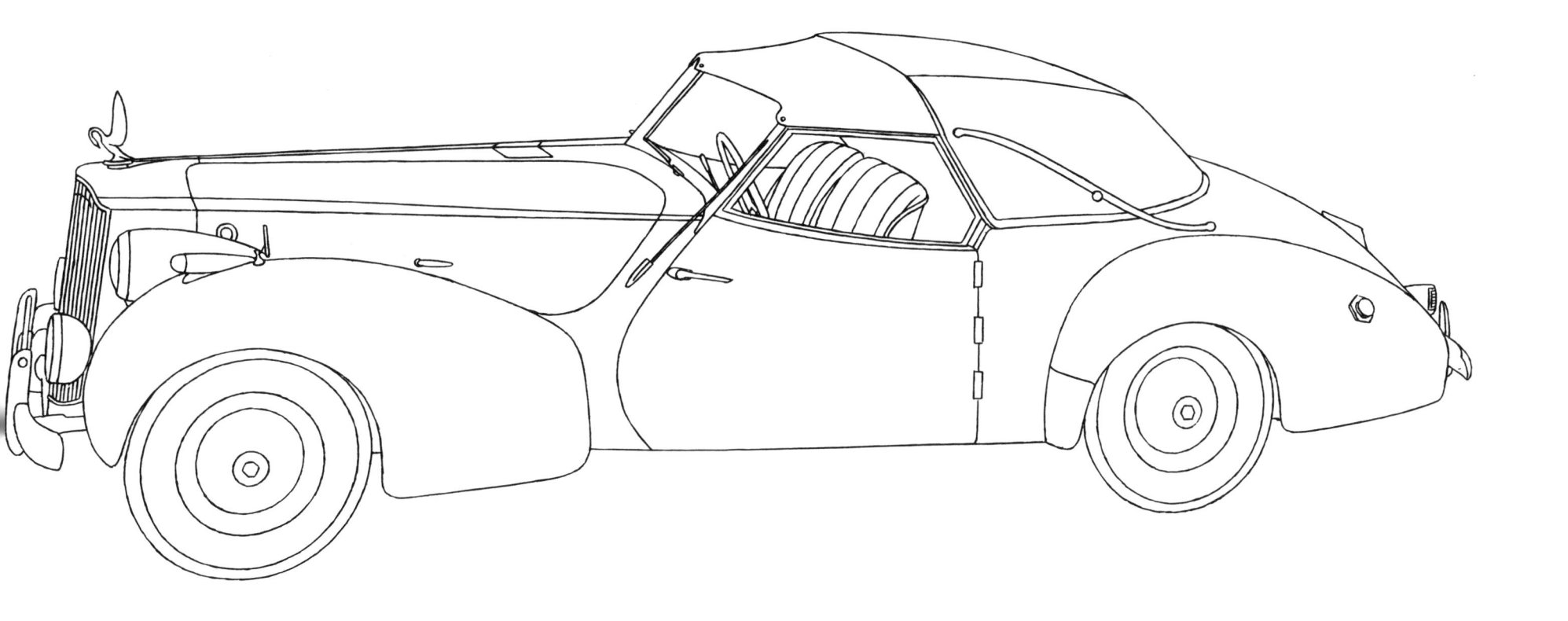

38. Packard, 1940. During the 1930s and early 40s, the Packard was probably the most widely distributed motorcar in the world. Like its British counterpart, Rolls-Royce, the American firm Packard believed that a car's most valuable assets were a smooth, quiet ride and reliable performance. This 1940-model Packard provided both. Its innovative "super 8" engine produced ample power to comfortably handle Packard's standard luxury bodies, as well as the large, sleekly styled, custom-built body shown here. Packard, after an unsuccessful merger with Studebaker in 1954, discontinued production in the United States in 1964.

39. Buick Limited, 1941. By 1940 the number of companies manufacturing luxury motorcars in the United States had dwindled drastically. General Motors, however, continued strong in the field, offering a variety of elegant, long-hooded automobiles produced by three of its top divisions: Cadillac, Oldsmobile and Buick. Buick produced the Limited, shown here in its 1941 form with a landaulette body. The landaulette was a style of limousine coachwork that had a flexible roof over the rear of the car that could be folded down to expose the back seats to the open air. Buick discontinued the Limited after the Second World War, leaving only Cadillac to handle General Motors' luxury line of specialized vehicles, Oldsmobile having withdrawn from the specialty market earlier.

40. Cadillac, 1941. A division of General Motors, Cadillac has long had a reputation for producing some of the world's most luxurious automobiles. In early 1941 the United States was not yet at war, and demand for the 1941-model Cadillac was high. After the United States entered the war, however, civilian automobile production was restricted as automotive factories turned their resources to the production of military vehicles, weapons and supplies. During the war, U.S. car manufacturers made almost twenty-nine billion dollars' worth of equipment in support of the Allied effort. This frontal view of the Cadillac shows the extent to which body design had changed by 1941. Previously distinct body parts were now part of the whole. Fenders and bumpers no longer looked as if they had been added on as an afterthought; headlamps were recessed into the fenders; and sidemounts were removed, the spare tire now in the trunk. The new alligator hood permitted shallower grilles that were as wide as they once were high.

41. 1100B Fiat, 1947. Fiat, an automotive giant in Italy and throughout Europe, was just as adept at manufacturing successful racing cars as it was at producing successful family cars. Advances made in the racing field paid off handsomely in engine efficiency when adapted to conventional motorcars. This 1947 1100B-model Fiat, though neither luxurious nor fast-looking, proved to be extremely popular with Italian car-buyers wanting superior performance and reliability, economical operation and a relatively low price. Like most cars built in the late 1940s, the 1100B was considered a new model but essentially was a warmed-over design from before the war. This sturdy compact did, however, feature a new V-shaped grille and a luggage rack that was attached to the back of the body, providing more space for the passengers inside.

42. XK 120 Jaguar, 1949. Unveiled at the 1948 London Motor Show, the XK 120 Jaguar caused an immediate stir: Here was a sleek, streamlined, two-seat sports car, with a 3.4-liter, 6-cylinder, 160-bhp engine, that could outperform cars costing two or three times the XK's price. Its introduction heralded the new age of the fast, relatively inexpensive postwar sports car. Yet for all its power, its ride, even at 125 mph, was smooth, quiet and comfortable, not to mention fun.

43. Bristol 401, 1949. This British-built sports car, introduced in 1949, is a closer ancestor of the modern sporting sedan than is the Jaguar XK. Unlike the two-seat XK, the 401 combined speed with a spacious, closed interior that could comfortably fit four adults. Moreover, its sleek, aerodynamic shape permitted fuel consumption of 25 mpg. However, a major drawback to most sports-car enthusiasts was its high price, equal to that of two Jaguars.

44. Saab Type 92, 1950. The only country that continued with any regularity to produce civilian motorcars during the Second World War was Sweden. However, prior to 1950, Sweden had only one national representative in the automotive industry: Volvo. In 1950, Saab, previously an aircraft manufacturer, entered the market and turned out 1,246 identical two-door sedans, all in the same shade of green. Even though it would be seven years before Saab became known outside of Scandinavia, its debut automobile was noteworthy. The Type 92 was a small, front-wheel-drive, aerodynamic sedan with independent suspension, hydraulic brakes and an economical, water-cooled, 764-cc engine. It offered a quiet ride, even at its top speed of 75 mph, and featured a fold-out locker located beneath the car's rear for storing the spare tire.

45. Fiat 1400, 1950. During the early 1950s, a time of economic stringency, various European car manufacturers introduced low-priced automobiles that were meant to appeal to the masses. Many of these motorcars were similar in that their styling was modeled on American sedans of the early 1940s. The Fiat 1400 typified these American-type cars. Its softly curved body, though neither luxurious nor elegant, was large enough to hold six people, provided good visibility and adequate room for luggage, and was mass-producible. Unfortunately it was also under-powered. In order to cut costs, Fiat had employed a 4-cylinder, 1.4-liter, 44-bhp engine in the 1400 model, not nearly enough engine to handle the 2,500-pound weight of the car comfortably. Although it was initially successful, the Fiat 1400, like most of the other "American compacts," could not compete for long on the world market against the likes of the Volkswagen Beetle and more powerful 6-cylinder cars. However, Fiat, the 1400 being just one of several models in production, easily continued to dominate Italy's automotive industry.

46. Citroën 11CV, 1953. The idea of having a door at the rear of a car goes all the way back to the "commercial sedans" produced by American and British manufacturers in the late 1920s and early 30s. The rear-door style was even more popular in France in the 1930s when just about every French maker of inexpensive cars offered a model with a fifth door at the back. These early ancestors of the modern station wagon and hatchback were usually 4-cylinder, long-chassis editions with room for seven or eight people, and often came with detachable rear seating. Unlike many earlier commercial sedans, the Citroën 11CV had sufficient power to cope with extra loads, and its entire tailgate swung upwards rather than sidewards as had earlier versions.